By Jane R. Davis

I0800064

History's very Worst

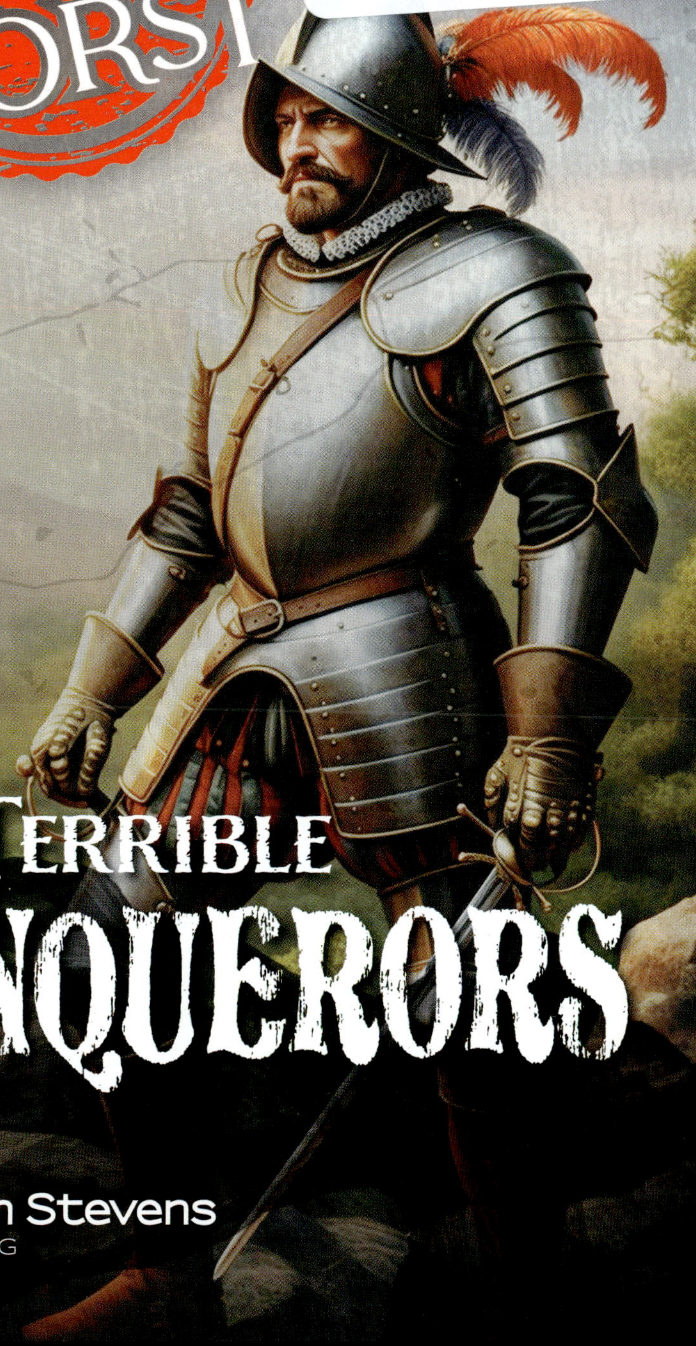

Ten Terrible Conquerors

Gareth Stevens Publishing

Please visit our website, www.garethstevens.com. For a free color catalog of all our high-quality books, call toll free 1-800-542-2595 or fax 1-877-542-2596.

Cataloging-in-Publication Data
Names: Davis, Jane R.
Title: Ten terrible conquerors / Jane R. Davis.
Description: Buffalo, NY : Gareth Stevens Publishing, 2026. | Series: History's very worst | Includes glossary and index.
Identifiers: ISBN 9781482472615 (pbk.) | ISBN 9781482472622 (library bound) | ISBN 9781482472639 (ebook)
Subjects: LCSH: Conquerors–History–Juvenile literature. | Conquerors–Biography--Juvenile literature. | History, Military–Juvenile literature. | War and civilization–Juvenile literature.
Classification: LCC D107.D28 2026 | DDC 321.0092′2–dc23

Published in 2026 by
Gareth Stevens Publishing
2544 Clinton Street
Buffalo, NY 14224

Copyright © 2026 Gareth Stevens Publishing

Designer: Tanya Dellaccio Keeney
Editor: Kristen Nelson

Photo credits: Cover Shutterstock AI/Shutterstock.com; p. 5 Only Fabrizio/Shutterstock.com; pp. 6, 27 Andreas Wolochow/Shutterstock.com; p. 7 miwuj/Shutterstock.com; pp. 8, 13 Mophart Creation/Shutterstock.com; p. 9 Courtesy of The Met; p. 11Shutterstock AI Generator/Shutterstock.com; p. 12 https://upload.wikimedia.org/wikipedia/commons/8/85/King_William_I_%28%27The_Conqueror%27%29_from_NPG.jpg; p. 14 https://upload.wikimedia.org/wikipedia/commons/3/35/YuanEmperorAlbumGenghisPortrait.jpg; pp. 15, Peter Hermes Furian/Shutterstock.com; p. 17 https://upload.wikimedia.org/wikipedia/commons/6/6b/Depiction_of_Timur_granting_audience_on_the_occasion_of_his_accession%2C_in_the_near_contemporary_Zafarnama_%281424-1428%29%2C_1467_edition.jpg; p. 18 Pyty/Shutterstock.com; p. 19 https://upload.wikimedia.org/wikipedia/commons/0/06/Retrato_de_Hern%C3%A1n_Cort%C3%A9s.jpg; p. 21, 29 Everett Collection/Shutterstock.com; p. 23 https://upload.wikimedia.org/wikipedia/commons/1/1e/Jacques-Louis_David_-_The_Coronation_of_Napoleon_%281805-1807%29.jpg; p. 25 https://upload.wikimedia.org/wikipedia/commons/5/50/Shaka_of_Zululand_statue_2015_London_%281%29.JPG.

Some of the images in this book illustrate individuals who are models. The depictions do not imply actual situations or events.

All rights reserved. No part of this book may be reproduced in any form without permission in writing from the publisher, except by a reviewer.

Printed in the United States of America

CPSIA compliance information: Batch #CSGS26 For further information contact Gareth Stevens, at 1-800-542-2595.

Find us on

CONTENTS

Words in the glossary appear in **bold** the first time they are used in the text.

WHO IS A CONQUEROR?

A conqueror is someone who travels to another land to take control of it. Some conquerors in history are remembered for their achievements, including their ability to take over a large area. Many are remembered for their terrible deeds as they conquered. They caused huge losses of life, used **brutal** military **tactics**, and did everything they could to stay in power.

From ancient history to more modern times, conquerors have risen to power around the world. Who was the most terrible? Read on and use what you learn to decide your answer!

Trajan was the emperor of ancient Rome that grew the empire to its largest. While he added land to the Roman Empire in his life, he is remembered for his fairness and building bridges, not the terrible things he may have done to gain the land.

ALEXANDER THE GREAT

Alexander the Great came to power in the ancient country of Macedonia when his father died in 336 BCE. The Macedonian army was fearsome—and Alexander put it to use.

Alexander is called "great" by historians in the Western Hemisphere, or half of Earth. In the Eastern Hemisphere in places where he conquered, he isn't remembered in such a positive light.

THE UGLY TRUTH

ALEXANDER CRUSHED A **REBELLION** IN THE GREEK CITY-STATE OF THEBES IN 335 BCE. HE LEFT THE CITY IN RUIN AND ENSLAVED ALMOST EVERYONE WHO LIVED THERE.

Alexander the Great is remembered as a great military mind. He succeeded in expanding his empire to include Egypt, Greece, and parts of the Middle East and Asia. But as his armies won battles, they also killed thousands of their enemies at his direction. And he wasn't always looking out for his own soldiers. One way he defeated the Persian King Darius III was by sacrificing thousands of his own troops.

JULIUS CAESAR

When Julius Caesar was born around 100 BCE, Rome was a **republic**. By the time he was killed by his rivals, it was becoming an empire headed by one powerful ruler, or dictator.

Caesar rose to power when he became a consul, or leader, in 59 BCE. He served for year and then headed to Gaul (modern France). He conquered the whole of Gaul and gained supporters. When he returned to Rome in 49 BCE, he brought an army. He fought the opposition and became Rome's dictator in 46 BCE.

Before he could truly grow Rome into an empire, Caesar was killed on March 15, 44 BCE.

Some leaders in Rome thought Caesar was already too powerful in 44 BCE. They worried what would happen if they didn't stop him when they had the chance.

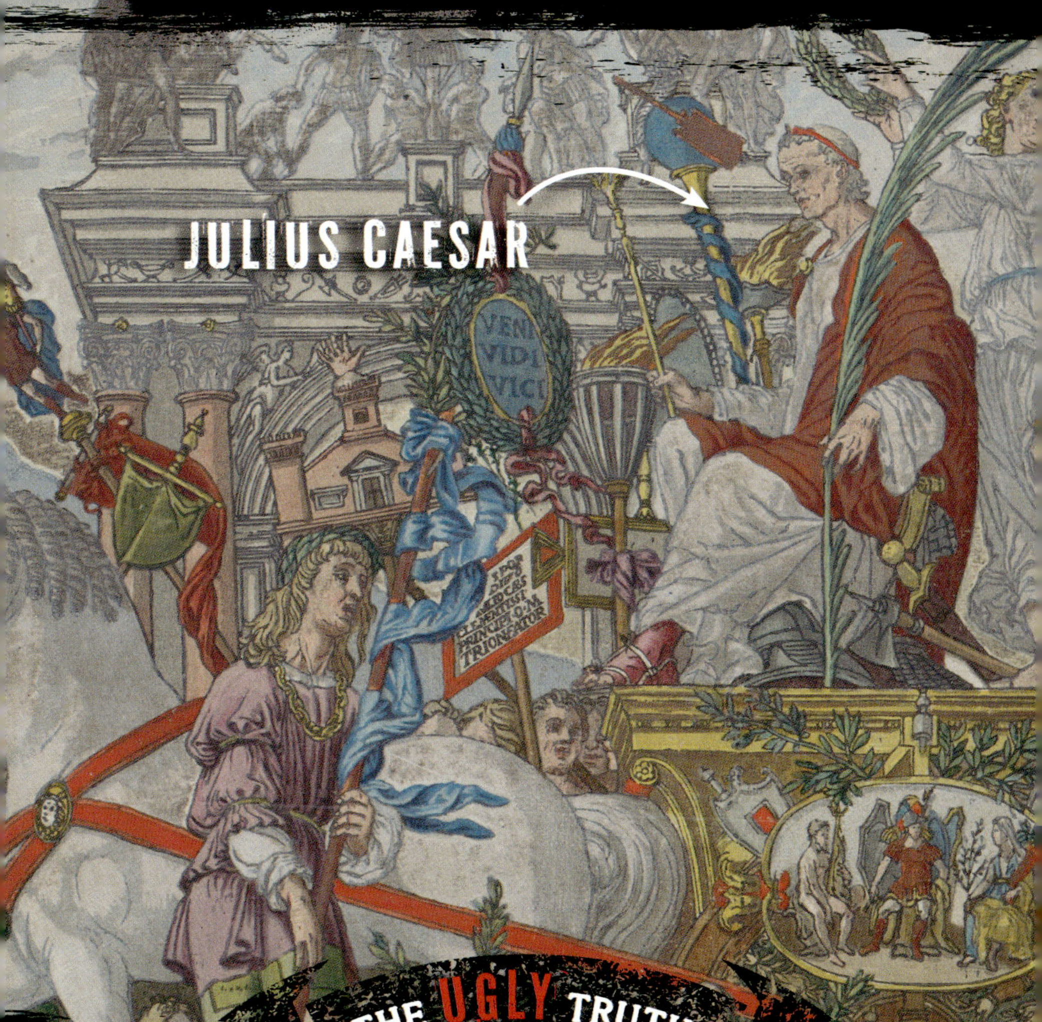

THE UGLY TRUTH

WHILE CONQUERING GAUL, CAESAR WAS **RUTHLESS**. IN ONE PLACE, HE CUT THE HANDS OFF ALL THOSE WHO SURVIVED HIS ATTACK.

ATTILA THE HUN

The Roman Empire split into two parts in 286 CE. The eastern Roman Empire, called the Byzantine Empire, was the stronger of the two. But, the Byzantine emperor was afraid of a certain man and his forces: Attila and the Huns he led. To avoid attack, the Byzantine emperor gave thousands of pounds of gold to the Huns.

Attila was known for destroying whole villages and leaving no one alive, among other terrible deeds done in the name of military conquest. In fact, when the Byzantine Empire missed paying the Huns, Attila struck, first in 441, then again in 447.

THE UGLY TRUTH

AT FIRST, ATTILA RULED ALONGSIDE HIS BROTHER. HE HAD HIS BROTHER KILLED AROUND 445.

Attila expanded the land controlled by the Huns. He **decimated** parts of the Byzantine Empire, but he never took its capital of Constantinople.

WILLIAM THE CONQUEROR

William was a nobleman from Normandy, France. He steadily gained more influence there in the 1060s. Then, his cousin, King Edward of England, died. William claimed he should now be the English king. Harold II took the throne though, and William readied to attack.

Harold II was killed during the Battle of Hastings, after which William the Conqueror (shown here) became king of England.

BATTLE OF HASTINGS

THE UGLY TRUTH

THE NORMAN SOLDIERS WERE KNOWN TO BE SO HARSH IN DEFEATING THOSE WHO OPPOSED THEM, THERE WAS A DROP IN THE NUMBER OF PEOPLE WHO LIVED IN ENGLAND IN THE FIRST PART OF WILLIAM'S REIGN.

William's invaded England with thousands of soldiers in 1066. He used bold military tactics, including a fake retreat, to defeat Harold II. William made himself the king—and used great force to put down anyone who rebelled.

William the Conqueror took land from the English nobles and gave it to his French supporters. His conquest and rule led to the **feudal system** in England.

GENGHIS KHAN

A young man named Temüjin unified the many groups of Mongols in central Asia around the year 1200. As he did so, he killed their leaders so no one would oppose him. His followers came to call him Genghis Khan, which means "emperor of all men."

THE UGLY TRUTH

GENGHIS KHAN'S HAD A **REPUTATION** FOR BRUTALITY, AND HIS ENEMIES **EXAGGERATED** IT FURTHER. THIS MADE IT EASIER FOR THE MONGOLS TO CONQUER. PEOPLE WOULD SOMETIMES JUST SURRENDER, OR GIVE UP, WITHOUT FIGHTING!

MONGOL EMPIRE AT THE TIME OF GENGHIS KHAN'S DEATH, 1227

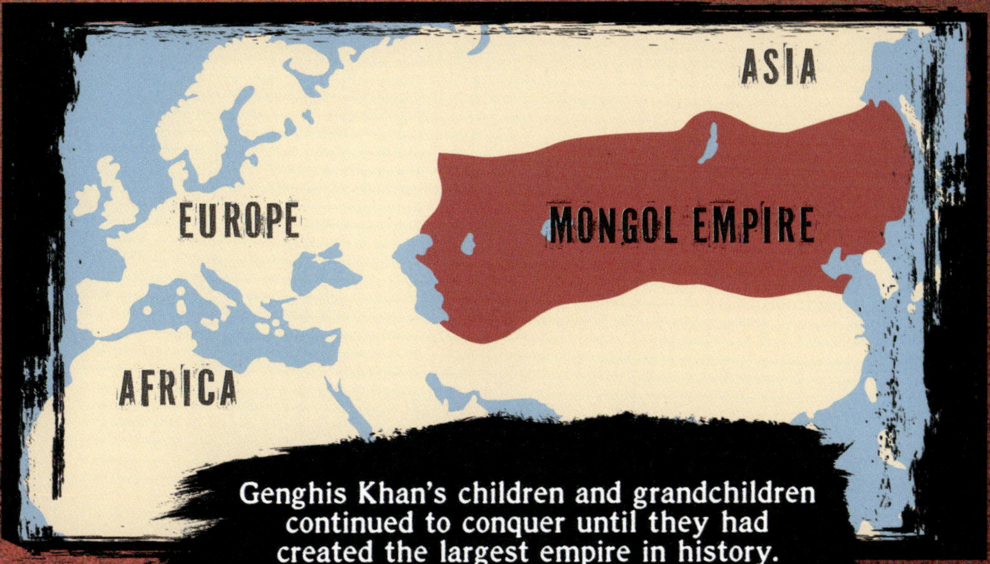

Genghis Khan's children and grandchildren continued to conquer until they had created the largest empire in history.

Genghis Khan's army set out to conquer lands beyond Mongolia. He first invaded China, likely killing millions. War with Khwárezm (today's Turkmenistan and Uzbekistan) further supported his terrible reputation. His forces destroyed cities, often putting to death everyone who lived there. Or, he used prisoners as the first troops in other battles, which meant they died anyway.

TIMUR

In the 1300s and early 1400s, Timur conquered land from India to Russia and from Mongolia to the Mediterranean Sea. This massive empire was formed through the destruction of cities, including Baghdad and Damascus and others that had ancient roots.

Timur was born in present-day Uzbekistan into one of the many groups of Mongols that came after Genghis Khan. Timur gained power using his military smarts. Like Genghis Khan, he led forces that likely killed millions of people as they conquered. Unlike Genghis Khan, Timur's empire didn't last long after his death. He didn't set up new governments after he destroyed an area.

THE UGLY TRUTH

WHEN TIMUR AND HIS ARMY TOOK BAGHDAD (IN MODERN IRAQ) IN 1401, THEY KILLED 20,000 PEOPLE THAT LIVED THERE.

Sometimes Timur is called Tamerlane or Tamberlane. This may have to do with an injured leg he had, or "Timur the lame."

HERNÁN CORTÉS

By conquering Mexico for Spain in the early 1500s, Hernán Cortés played a part in shaping the history of North America. He also decimated almost an entire culture in the process.

THE UGLY TRUTH

CORTÉS AND HIS MEN BROUGHT THE DISEASE SMALLPOX TO THE AZTEC. AZTEC PEOPLE KILLED BY SMALLPOX SOON FILLED THE STREETS OF THE SPANISH-HELD TENOCHTITLÁN.

It took Cortés less than two years to topple the Aztec Empire, which had been in power for almost 200 years!

Cortés first came to Mexico in 1519 after being part of the Spanish forces conquering the island of Cuba. He wanted to claim land for Spain, convert Native peoples to Christianity, and make his fortune. His expedition wasn't large. He only had 100 men. However, they defeated Native groups as they headed to the Aztec city of Tenochtitlán.

Once there, Cortés captured Emperor Moctezuma II and tried to rule—while holding the emperor prisoner!

Napoleon Bonaparte

Napoleon Bonaparte rose through the ranks of the French military during the late 1700s. He became known for smart **strategy** and winning on the battlefield. But there was unrest in France at the time. In 1792, the French people overthrew the king. Two years later they overthrew another leader.

Napoleon fought for the new government that followed. He became a French hero as he took on the country's enemies. Napoleon used his military reputation to become the first consul, or top leader, of France in 1799. He found ways to take out his political rivals as well as gain popularity with the people of France.

Napoleon used newspaper articles, paintings, and other communication to exaggerate his military might and improve his image.

Napoleon wanted even more power. He worked to expand France into an empire by invading many countries in Western Europe. To the French, this was heroic. To the invaded lands, Napoleon was a terrible conqueror who used great force to steal what he wanted—land and resources.

In 1804, Napoleon crowned himself the emperor of France. He continued to defeat European powers like Germany and Italy. Then, in 1812 he tried to invade the huge country of Russia in winter. His troops were unprepared for cold conditions, and Napoleon was defeated. Not long after, Napoleon fell from power in Europe.

THE UGLY TRUTH

MANY OF NAPOLEON'S TROOPS DIDN'T MAKE IT TO ANY BATTLES IN RUSSIA. THEY **STARVED** IN THE TERRIBLE COLD OF THE RUSSIAN WINTER.

This famous painting shows Napoleon crowning his wife Joséphine after his own coronation, or crowning.

SHAKA

During the early 1800s in South Africa, Native South Africans lived in clans, or groups. Shaka rose to power in the Zulu clan in 1816. The clan was small, but Shaka killed anyone who opposed him. Then, he trained and organized his army—and set out to conquer those near him, starting around 1818.

Shaka directed his forces to wipe out the other clans they fought. When there were survivors, they joined the Zulu. Many people fled the region too. Shaka's 10 years as leader of the Zulu led to the death of as many as a million people.

THE UGLY TRUTH

WHEN SHAKA FIRST BEGAN WARRING WITH NEARBY CLANS, HE RUTHLESSLY KILLED MEN WHO HAD WRONGED HIM IN THE PAST. HE **IMPALED** THEM ON THEIR OWN FENCES.

Shaka was killed by his half-brothers in September 1828.

ADOLF HITLER

World War I was a conflict between many countries that occurred from 1914 to 1918. The treaty that ended that war blamed Germany and its **allies**. Germany was treated harshly. Its economy suffered and many German people were angry.

It was during this time that Adolf Hitler and the Nazi party came to power. Hitler was named chancellor of Germany in 1933. He aimed to restore Germany to glory as well as conquer Europe. The first country he invaded was Poland in 1939. When Great Britian and France declared war on Germany, World War II had begun.

THE UGLY TRUTH

HITLER AND HIS SUPPORTERS WANTED TO CREATE A "PURE" GERMAN NATION. THEY WANTED TO WIPE OUT THE JEWISH PEOPLE, AMONG OTHER GROUPS.

Hitler commanded any room he spoke in. He held huge rallies that gave Germans hope that Hitler could restore their country.

At Hitler's direction, German forces invaded and occupied Demark, Belgium, Norway, France, the Netherlands, Luxembourg, Yugoslavia, and Greece. His Nazi party also set up concentration camps across Germany and other places in Europe. About 6 million Jewish people and millions of others were killed in these camps.

Like the conquerors who came before him, Hitler was responsible for many deaths. Historians continue to look back on these powerful leaders. They study how they took control of armies, governments, and conquered land. In this way, we can all learn from what has come before us—and try to stop the most terrible of it from happening again.

THE UGLY TRUTH

CONCENTRATION CAMPS ARE PLACES WHERE MANY PEOPLE ARE IMPRISONED. THEY HAVE NOT BROKEN THE LAW BUT ARE BEING HELD BECAUSE THEY OPPOSE THOSE IN POWER OR BECAUSE THEY HAVE A CERTAIN BACKGROUND OR BELIEFS, SUCH AS BEING JEWISH.

Hitler died in 1945 when troops entered the German city of Berlin, sealing the defeat of the Nazis and Hitler. It is likely he shot himself.

GLOSSARY

ally: One of two or more people or groups who work together.

brutal: Especially violent or severe.

decimate: To cause great destruction or harm to.

exaggerate: To think of or describe something as larger or greater than it really is.

feudal system: A political set up in which vassals paid a lord and worked their land in order to be protected.

impale: To cause a pointed object to go into or through something or someone.

rebellion: A fight to overthrow a government.

republic: A form of government in which the people elect representatives who run the government.

reputation: The views that are held about something or someone.

ruthless: Cruel.

starve: To die from hunger.

strategy: A carefully thought-out plan.

tactic: A method for accomplishing a military goal.

FOR MORE INFORMATION

BOOKS

Davis, Kenneth C. *Strongman: The Rise of Five Dictators and the Fall of Democracy*. New York, NY: Square Fish/Henry Holt and Company, 2022.

Gunderson, Jessica. *Conquistadors.* Mankato, MN: Creative Education and Creative Paperbacks, 2025.

Paparchontis, Kathy. *100 World Leaders Who Shaped World History*. Naperville, IL: Sourebooks Explore, 2023.

WEBSITES

Adolf Hitler
https://kids.britannica.com/kids/article/Adolf-Hitler/353254
Read more about Hitler's life and rise to power in Germany in the 1930s.

William I "The Conqueror"
https://www.royal.uk/william-the-conqueror
Read more details about William the Conqueror on the official website of the British monarchy.

Publisher's note to educators and parents: Our editors have carefully reviewed this website to ensure it is suitable for students. Many websites change frequently, however, and we cannot guarantee that a site's future contents will continue to meet our high standards of quality and educational value. Be advised that students should be closely supervised whenever they access the internet.

INDEX